КОЛОКОЛА.

Слова ЭДГАРА ПОЭ перев. БАЛЬМО[

I.

Слышишь, сани мчатся въ рядъ,
  Мчатся въ рядъ.
  Колокольчики звенятъ,   [томятъ,
Серебристымъ легкимъ звономъ, слухъ нашъ сладостно
Этимъ пѣньемъ и гудѣньемъ о забвеньи говорятъ.
  О, какъ звонко, звонко, звонко,
  Точно звучный смѣхъ ребенка,
  Въ ясномъ воздухѣ ночномъ
  Говорятъ они о томъ,
  Что за днями заблужденья
  Наступаетъ возрожденье,   [сномъ.
Что волшебно наслажденье, наслажденье нѣжнымъ
  Сани мчатся, мчатся въ рядъ,
  Колокольчики звенятъ,
Звѣзды слушаютъ, какъ сани, убѣгая, говорятъ,
  И, внимая имъ, горятъ,
И мечтая, и блистая, въ небѣ духами парятъ;
  И измѣнчивымъ сіяньемъ,
  Молчаливымъ обаяньемъ,   [говорятъ.
Вмѣстѣ съ звономъ, вмѣстѣ съ пѣньемъ, о забвеньи

II.

  Слышишь, къ свадьбѣ зовъ святой,
    Золотой.
Сколько нѣжнаго блаженства въ этой пѣснѣ молодой!
  Сквозь спокойный воздухъ ночи
  Словно смотрятъ чьи-то очи,
    И блестятъ,
Изъ волны пѣвучихъ звуковъ на луну они глядятъ.
  Изъ призывныхъ дивныхъ келій,
  Полны сказочныхъ веселій,
Наростая, упадая, брызги свѣтлыя летятъ.
  Вновь потухнутъ, вновь блестятъ,
  И роняютъ свѣтлый взглядъ   [сновъ,
На грядущее, гдѣ дремлетъ безмятежность нѣжныхъ
Возвѣщаемыхъ согласьемъ золотыхъ колоколовъ.

III.

  Слышишь, воющій набатъ,
  Точно стонетъ мѣдный адъ.
Эти звуки, въ дикой мукѣ, сказку ужасовъ твердятъ.
  Точно молятъ имъ помочь,
  Крикъ кидаютъ прямо въ ночь,
  Прямо въ уши темной ночи
  Каждый звукъ,
  То длиннѣе, то короче,
  Возвѣщаетъ свой испугъ, —
  И испугъ ихъ такъ великъ,
  Такъ безуменъ каждый крикъ,
Что разорванные звоны, неспособные звучать,
Могутъ только биться, биться и кричать, кри-
  Только плакать о пощадѣ, [чать, кричать.
  И къ пылающей громадѣ

  Вопли скорби обра
  А межъ тѣмъ огонь
  И глухой и многошумный,
    Все горитъ,
  То изъ оконъ, то на крышѣ,
  Мчится выше, выше, выше,
  И какъ будто говоритъ:
    Я хочу
Выше мчаться, разгораться, встрѣчу лунному лучу,
Иль умру, иль тотчасъ, тотчасъ вплоть до мѣсяца взлечу.
  О, набатъ, набатъ, набатъ,
  Если бъ ты вернулъ назадъ
Этотъ ужасъ, это пламя, эту искру, этотъ взглядъ,
  Этотъ первый взглядъ огня,
О которомъ ты вѣщаешь, съ воплемъ, съ плачемъ и
  А теперь намъ нѣтъ спасенья, [звеня.
  Всюду пламя и кипѣнье,
  Всюду страхъ и возмущенье.
  Твой призывъ,
  Дикихъ звуковъ несогласность
  Возвѣщаетъ намъ опасность,
То растетъ бѣда глухая, то спадаетъ, какъ приливъ.
Слухъ нашъ чутко ловитъ волны въ перемѣнѣ звуковой,
Вновь спадаетъ, вновь рыдаетъ мѣдно-стонущій прибой!

IV.

  Похоронный слышенъ звонъ,
    Долгій звонъ!   [сонъ.
Горькой скорби, слышны звуки, горькой жизни конченъ
Звукъ желѣзный возвѣщаетъ, о печали похоронъ.
  И невольно мы дрожимъ,
  Отъ забавъ своихъ спѣшимъ,
И рыдаемъ, вспоминаемъ, что и мы глаза смежимъ.
  Неизмѣнно-монотонный,
  Этотъ возгласъ отдаленный,
  Похоронный тяжкій звонъ,
    Точно стонъ,
   Скорбный, гнѣвный,
   И плачевный,
  Выростаетъ въ долгій гулъ.   [нулъ.
Возвѣщаетъ, что страдалецъ, непробуднымъ сномъ ус-
  Въ колокольныхъ кельяхъ ржавыхъ,
  Онъ для правыхъ и неправыхъ
  Грозно вторитъ объ одномъ: [сномъ.
Что на сердцѣ будетъ камень, что глаза сомкнутся
  Факелъ траурный горитъ,
Съ колокольни кто-то крикнулъ, кто-то громко гово-
  Кто-то черный тамъ стоитъ. [ритъ,
  И хохочетъ, и гремитъ,
  И гудитъ, гудитъ, гудитъ,
  Къ колокольнѣ припадаетъ,
  Гулкій колоколъ качаетъ,
  Гулкій колоколъ рыдаетъ,
  Стонетъ въ воздухѣ нѣмомъ
И протяжно возвѣщаетъ, о покоѣ гробовомъ.

Deutsch von BERTHOLD FEIWEL
nach der Übertragung ins Russische von K. BALMONT.

I.

Hörst du? Schlitten, windesschnell,
Windesschnell,
Schellenglöckchen klingeln hell,
Mit dem silberfeinen Schwingen
Weich das Ohr umstreicheln sie,
Mit dem Singen, mit dem Klingen
„Sollst vergessen!" schmeicheln sie.
O wie lieblich hallt es, hallt es,
Wie ein Kinderlachen schallt es,
In dem Odem klarer Nacht
Sprechen Glöckchenstimmen sacht:
Nach der Zeit des Irregehens,
Naht der Tag des Auferstehens,
Kommt die Lust des Ganz-Vergehens
In des Schlafes süßer Macht.
Schlitten-Flirren windesschnell,
Schellen-Klingeln silberhell,
Und die Sterne droben, lauschend
Der Enteilenden Gesang,
Glühen auf im Sehnsuchtsdrang,
Und sie träumen, und sie säumen
Geistergleich, im Strahlengold,
Und aus ihrem Wunderflimmern,
Aus dem schweigend-tiefen Schimmern,
Eins dem Singen
Eins dem Klingen
„Sollst vergessen!" tönt es hold.

II.

Hörst du? „Hochzeit" tönt's entlang,
Goldner Klang!
Wieviel Zärtlichkeit und Inbrunst
In dem heil'gen Jugendsang!
Wie wenn träumend Augen schauen
Auf zum Himmelszelt, dem blauen,
Strahlend ganz,
Aus der Klänge reinem Wogen
Zu des lichten Mondes Glanz.
Aus der Macht und Pracht der Zellen
Voll der Lust, der wunderhellen,
Jetzt im Steigen, jetzt im Neigen,
Schwebt der holden Klänge Tanz.
Bald erlöschend, bald voll Glut,
Und ergießt des Lichtes Flut
Auf ein Zukunftsbild, wo lieblich

Keusche Träume ruhn zur Stund,
Die harmonisch-rein verkündet
Goldnen Tons der Glocken Mund.

III.

Hörst du, tobendes Gedröhn,
Gleichwie erznen Schlunds Gestöhn.
Banger Trauer Schmerz und Schauer
Wiederholt dies Schreckgetön.
Wie ein Flehen: „Helft, herbei!"
Füllt's die Nacht mit Schrei um Schrei,
Füllt's die taube Nacht mit Wehe,
Jedes Schrein,
Bald getrag'ner und bald jähe,
Klagt ins Dunkel seine Pein.
Und die Qual ist also groß,
Jeder Schrei so fassungslos,
Daß die ganz verworr'nen Töne,
Nicht imstand mehr Klang zu sein,
Nur noch irren, holpern, stolpern
Und nur schrein, nur schrein, nur
schrein,
Nur Erbarmen flehn und weinen
Und den grellen Flammenscheinen
Jammernd künden höchste Pein.
Doch indes der Brand, der tolle,
Dumpfe Brand, der schreckensvolle
Stetig schwillt.
Jetzt durchs Fenster, jetzt ganz oben,
Höher, höher Flammen toben,
Und es ist als spräch' es wild:
„Ja, ich will,
Hoch mich windend, neu entzündend
An des Mondes lichter Flut,
Sei's vergehn, sei's jetzt und jetzt
schon
Ganz hinauf zur Mondesglut".
O Gedröhn, Gedröhn, Gedröhn,
O verstummte dies Getön,
Dies Entsetzen, diese Flammen, diese
Gluten — und dies Bild,
Dieses Feuers erstes Bild,
Das du überallhin meldest
Klagend, jammernd, hallend-wild.
Aber jetzt gibt's kein Erhören,
Ringsum flammendes Zerstören,

Ringsum Schrecken und Empören!
Feuerschrei,
Deine Rufe wild-zerfahren
Künden gellend uns Gefahren,
Einmal wächst die Not, die dumpfe,
Dann verebbt die Raserei.
Und das Ohr lauscht bang dem Wechsel
Jedes Tons und jedes Klangs,
Jetzt dem Fallen, jetzt dem Schwellen
Ehern-hohlen Wellengangs.

IV.

Horch, es dröhnet Grabesklang,
Dumpf und bang,
Bitt're Trübsal hallet wider,
Bitt'ren Lebens Traum versank,
Und die Eisenzungen künden
Von dem bittern letzten Gang!
Unwillkürlich stockt der Fuß,
Alle Lust wird Überdruß,
Jähes Trauern läßt dich schauern,
Daß auch dein Aug' brechen muß.
Dieses quälerische, stumpfe,
Langgezogene und dumpfe,
Monotone Grabgedröhn,
Dies Gestöhn,
Peinlich, grollend, voller Klagen,
Wächst sich aus zu hohlem Schrei,
Laut verkündend, daß der Büßer
Ew'gem Schlaf verfallen sei.
Aus den rostig-roten Mündern
So den Frommen wie den Sündern
Drohend dröhnt es hart und fest:
Daß ein Stein sich legt aufs Herze,
Schwarze Nacht die Augen preßt.
Rauch aus Trauerfackeln schwillt,
Einer schreit vom Glockenturme,
Einer ruft von dorther wild,
— Welch ein düstres Schreckensbild! —
Wie er lacht, als ob er höhnt,
Und er dröhnt, er dröhnt, er dröhnt!
Nun im Turm mit irrem Springen
Jäh die Glocke läßt er schwingen,
Läßt die Glocke schluchzend klingen,
Stöhnend in die taube Luft,
Und getragne Kunde bringen
Von der Ruh in tiefer Gruft.

Sergei
RACHMANINOFF
THE BELLS
Choral Symphony
Op. 35

Vocal Score
Klavierauszug

PETRUCCI LIBRARY PRESS

Russian Poem by K. BALMONT adapted from "The Bells" by E. A. POE.

English translation by FANNY S. COPELAND.

I.

Listen, hear the silver bells!
   Silver bells!
   Hear the sledges with the bells,   [compels,
How they charm our weary senses with a sweetness that
In the ringing and the singing that of deep oblivion tells.
   Hear them calling, calling, calling,
   Rippling sounds of laughter, falling
   On the icy midnight air;
   And a promise they declare,
   That beyond Illusion's cumber,
   Births and lives beyond all number,   [pare.
Waits an universal slumber—deep and sweet past all com-
   Hear the sledges with the bells,
   Hear the silver-throated bells;   [foretells,
See, the stars bow down to hearken, what their melody
   With a passion that compels,   [hales,
And their dreaming is a gleaming that a perfumed air ex-
   And their thoughts are but a shining,
   And a luminous divining   [foretells.
Of the singing and the ringing, that a dreamless peace

II.

   Hear the mellow wedding bells,
      Golden bells!   [foretells!
What a world of tender passion their melodious voice
   Through the night their sound entrances,
   Like a lover's yearning glances,
      That arise
On a wave of tuneful rapture to the moon within the skies.
   From the sounding cells upwinging
   Flash the tones of joyous singing   [throats
Rising, falling, brightly calling; from a thousand happy
   Roll the glowing, golden notes,
   And an amber twilight gloats   [foretells,
While the tender vow is whispered that great happiness
To the rhyming and the chiming of the bells, the golden
         [bells!

III.

   Hear them, hear the brazen bells,
   Hear the loud alarum bells!   [dwells!
In their sobbing, in their throbbing what a tale of horror
   How beseeching sounds their cry
   'Neath the naked midnight sky,
   Trough the darkness wildly pleading
   In affright,
   Now approaching, now receding
   Rings their message through the night.
   And so fierce is their dismay
   And the terror they portray,   [only speak
That the brazen domes are riven, and their tongues can
In a tuneless, jangling wrangling as they shriek, and shriek,
   Till their frantic supplication   [and shriek,
   To the ruthless conflagration
   Grows discordant, faint and weak.

   But the fire sweeps on unheeding,
   And in vain is all their pleading
      With the flames!
   From each window, roof and spire,
   Leaping higher, higher, higher,
   Every lambent tongue proclaims:
      I shall soon,
Leaping higher, still aspire, till I reach the crescent moon;
Else I die of my desire in aspiring to the moon!
   O despair, despair, despair,
   That so feebly ye compare   [glare,
With the blazing, raging horror, and the panic, and the
   That ye cannot turn the flames,   [claims.
As your unavailing clang and clamour mournfully pro-
   And in hopeless resignation
   Man must yield his habitation
   To the warring desolation!
   Yet we know
   By the booming and the clanging,
   By the roaring and the twanging,   [flow.
How the danger falls and rises like the tides that ebb and
And the progress of the danger every ear distinctly tells
By the sinking and the swelling in the clamour of the bells.

IV.

   Hear the tolling of the bells,
      Mournful bells!   [tells!
Bitter end to fruitless dreaming their stern monody fore-
What a world of desolation in their iron utterance dwells!
   And we tremble at our doom,
   As we think upon the tomb,   [gloom.
Glad endeavour quenched for ever in the silence and the
   With persistent iteration
   They repeat their lamentation,
   Till each muffled monotone
   Seems a groan,
   Heavy, moaning,
   Their intoning,
   Waxing sorrowful and deep,   [sleep.
Bears the message, that a brother passed away to endless
   Those relentless voices rolling
   Seem to take a joy in tolling
   For the sinner and the just   [turned to dust
That their eyes be sealed in slumber, and their hearts be
   Where they lie beneath a stone.
But the spirit of the belfry is a sombre fiend that dwells
   In the shadow of the bells,
   And he gibbers, and he yells,
   As he knells, and knells, and knells,
   Madly round the belfry reeling,
   While the giant bells are pealing,
   While the bells are fiercely thrilling,
   Moaning forth the word of doom,
   While those iron bells, unfeeling,
   Through the void repeat the doom:
There is neither rest nor respite, save the quiet of the tomb!

CONTENTS

ORCHESTRA

3 flutes, piccolo, 3 oboes, English horn,

3 clarinets, bass clarinet, 3 bassoons, contrabassoon

6 horns, 3 trumpets, 3 trombones, tuba

timpani, triangle, tambourine, side drum, cymbals

glockenspiel, celesta, harp, piano

Violin I, Violin II, Viola, Violoncello, Bass

Duration: ca. 37 minutes

First performance: February 8, 1914
Moscow, Philharmonic Society Concert
Vocal soli, chorus and orchestra directed by the composer

This score is an unabridged, digitally-enhanced reissue of the vocal score originally published in 1920 by A. Gutheil, Moscow (plate A. 9719 G.).

ISBN: 1-978-60874-115-1
First Printing: July, 2013

КОЛОКОЛА.   GLOCKEN.
THE BELLS.

Op. 35.

Слова Эдгара Поэ. Пер. Бальмонта.
Gedicht von Edgar Poe.
Übersetzt von Berthold Feiwel nach der Übertragung
ins Russische von K. Balmont.
English translation of Balmont's poem
by Fanny S. Copeland.

Музыка С. Рахманинова
Musik von S. Rachmaninov
Klavierauszug von A. Goldenweiser

I.

II.

82

жен _ ства въ э _ той пѣс _ _ _ _ _ _ _ нѣ мо _ ло

In _ brunst in dem heil _ _ _ _ _ _ _ gen Ju _ gend

pas _ sion their me _ lo _ _ _ _ _ _ _ dious voice fore _

85 **41** **Più mosso.**

дой.

sang!

tells.

88

91

94

III.

255 [80]

чу.
Flut.
moon.

255
Fl.Cl.
f Piano
f Corni
[80]

258
mf cresc.
Иль
seis
Else
ум
rer
l

258
etc.
cresc.

въ пе - ре - мѣ - нѣ зву - ко - вой,
je - des Tons und je - des Klangs,
ev' - ry ear dis - tinct - ly tells.

въ пе - ре - мѣ - нѣ зву - ко - вой,
je - des Tons und je - des Klangs,
ev' - ry ear dis - tinct - ly tells.

IV.

Воз_вѣ_
*Laut ver_*
Bears the

ща_ет, что стра_да_лецъ не_про_буд_нымъ сномъ ус_нулъ.
kün_ det's, daß der Büs_ ser ew'_gem Schlaf ver_ fal_ len sei.
message that a bro_ ther passed a_way to end_ less sleep.

Tempo I.

La bouche fermée

Гул - кій ко - локолъ ры - да - етъ,
Jäh die Glok - ke läßt er klin - gen,
While those i - ron bells, un - feel - ing

Сто - нетъ въ воз - ду - хѣ нѣ - момъ
stöh - nend in die tau - be Luft,
through ___ the void re - peat the doom:

И про - тяж - но воз - вѣ -
und ge - trag - ne Kun - de
There is neith - er rest nor

ща - етъ о по - ко - ѣ гро - бо - вомъ.
brin - gen, von der Ruh in tie - fer Gruft.
res - pite, save the qui - et of the tomb.